Experiencing A Lasting and Fulfilling Marital Union

Dr. Kayode Ajimatanrareje Sr.

EXPERIENCING A LASTING & FULFILLING MARITAL UNION

DR. KAYODE AJIMATANRAREJE SR.

Essence

PUBLISHING

Belleville, Ontario, Canada

2009

Experiencing a Lasting and Fulfilling Marital Union

Copyright © 2009, Dr. Kayode Ajimatanrareje

All Scripture quotations, unless otherwise specified, are from *The Holy Bible, New International Version.* Copyright © 1973, 1978, 1984 International Bible Society. Used by permission of Zondervan Publishing House. All rights reserved. • Scripture quotations marked NKJV are taken from the New King James Version. Copyright © 1979, 1980, 1982. Thomas Nelson Inc., Publishers. • Scripture quotations marked KJV are from *The Holy Bible, King James Version.* Copyright © 1977, 1984, Thomas Nelson Inc., Publishers. • Scripture quotations marked NASB are taken from the *New American Standard Bible*, copyright © The Lockman Foundation 1960, 1962, 1963, 1968, 1971, 1972, 1973. All rights reserved.

Library and Archives Canada Cataloguing in Publication

Ajimatanrareje, Kayode
    Experiencing a lasting & fulfilling marital union / Kayode Ajimatanrareje, Sr.

Includes bibliographical references.
ISBN 978-1-55452-350-4

    1. Marriage--Religious aspects--Christianity. 2. Marriage--Biblical teaching. 3. Spouses--Religious life. I. Title.

BV4596.M3 A45 2009   248.8'44   C2008-908081-5

Essence Publishing is a Christian Book Publisher dedicated to furthering the work of Christ through the written word. For more information, contact: 20 Hanna Court, Belleville, Ontario, Canada K8P 5J2.

Phone: 1-800-238-6376. Fax: (613) 962-3055.
E-mail: info@essence-publishing.com
Web site: www.essence-publishing.com

This book is dedicated to
the wife of my youth,
Minister Olajumoke Ajimatanrareje,
and to the institution of marriage and family,
as ordained by the Almighty God.

Table of Contents

In the Image of God
One Flesh
    The Permanent Character of Marriage
    The Covenant Character of Marriage
Submit to One Another
    A Description of Marriage
    Made for Companionship: A Significant Purpose
    of Marriage
    Wholesome Sexual Fulfillment and Procreation

Foreword

My wife and I married in October of 1949 with no premarital counseling. I'm not too sure it would have been available had we requested it. Only the Lord knows how much we needed it. But that's all in the past, and thanks to His marvelous grace, we're on our way to our 59th anniversary. On a sad note, less than 5 per cent of the married couples in our country ever make it to their 55th.

Our first of four children came to us in 1951. I can't tell you how many mistakes we've made down through the years, and I'm sure we're not alone. We can honestly say most of those mistakes and errors were made out of sheer ignorance. Nor can I tell you how many times during all these years we have commented to each other how different it would have been for us had there been ministries like Focus on the Family or Christian books and magazines. They are available in abundant numbers today. Books, tapes, videos, radio, television. How thankful we are for all of these helps.

But in spite of these tools, most surveys and studies indicate that marriages and family living is almost in a trend towards meltdown. For years it's been common knowledge that the ugly 50 per cent divorce rate is just as high among Christians as it is in the non-Christian population of our country. There seems to be no indication that the trend of unmarried couples living together will ever decrease. In our young married years, in the fifties and sixties, my wife and I didn't know of one couple living together as though they were married. Now it's becoming more prevalent and common everyday. The biblical term for that lifestyle is *adultery* and yet one hardly hears the term used today. Now the terms are subtle: "relationship" or "my significant other" or even "an item." Not only are these trends bad, but their commonality and acceptability is reflecting a sad condition, not only in our country, but also in the Body of Christ, those of us who call ourselves "Christians."

I believe the people we call "Israel, God's chosen people," have been and will continue to be in a state of discipline by God. The reasons are many, but one is spelled out clearly and succinctly in Malachi 2:13-16 (NLT):

> *Here is another thing you do. You cover the Lord's altar with tears, weeping and groaning because he pays no attention to your offerings and doesn't accept them with pleasure. You cry out, "Why doesn't the Lord accept my worship?" I'll tell you why! Because*

the Lord witnessed the vows you and your wife made when you were young. But you have been unfaithful to her, though she remained your faithful partner, the wife of your marriage vows. Didn't the Lord make you one with your wife? In body and spirit you are his. And what does he want? Godly children from your union. So guard your heart; remain loyal to the wife of your youth. "For I hate divorce!" says the Lord, the God of Israel. "To divorce your wife is to overwhelm her with cruelty," says the Lord of Heaven's Armies. "So guard your heart; do not be unfaithful to your wife."

And so, we have before us, yet another book! I am not here suggesting it is the answer to the tragic state of marriage and family affairs with which we are confronted—no, not at all. But it certainly could be an answer. And why not another book? It could well be that this book, like the many others we have available to us, will touch your life or maybe that of your son or your daughter. How wonderful would that be!

You will find this book a very valuable tool—a wonderful, thoughtful and scripturally well-documented work from a gifted writer and a man who walks by faith.

Samuel and I became friends while he was attending Christian Heritage College in El Cajon, a suburb of San Diego in Southern California. As the pastor of First Baptist Church, Lemon Grove, Southern California, I had, at the time, the privilege of helping him matriculate with a scholarship at the California Baptist University in Riverside. After his graduation with a bachelor's degree in Psychology, he moved his growing family to the San Francisco area where he attended Golden Gate Baptist Theological Seminary, earning Master of Divinity and Doctor of Ministry degrees.

I commend this study, this labor of love from the heart of a man who is a dear friend and a brother in the Lord—a man who deeply loves Jesus Christ and His word. I pray that God will bless and use this valuable tool in your life and in the lives of your friends and family.

Rev. Robert E. Kleinschmidt

About the Author

Dr. Kayode Ajimatanrareje Sr. is an insightful preacher, teacher and marriage and family counselor. He is the author of *Make Disciple of All Nations: A Handbook for Authentic Christian Ministry*. He has also authored several articles, twenty devotional thoughts and gospel tracts for personal evangelism.

He is the pastor and General Overseer of Victory Christian Fellowship Ministries in the United States and Nigeria, West Africa. He is heard every week on the radio program "Victory Hour" in Nigeria on positive FM station, Akure, Ondo State. This unique radio program is undoubtedly touching many lives today, and God deserves all the glory.

Dr. Kayode has brought hope, freshness, comfort and restoration to many homes and marriages through his dynamic marriage conferences and years of marriage and family counseling. This book is indeed a product of his years of prayers and aspiration for the well-being of Christian marriages and families.

Dr. Kayode and his wife Olajumoke live in Pinole, California, and minister with their sons Kayode Jr., Sola and Tomi in Oakland, California.

Prologue

Marriage as ordained by God is undoubtedly the most important relationship on earth. Unfortunately, many married people in our contemporary world seem to be gliding through life without peace, harmony and joy. They lack meaning, purpose, and excitement. They are unhappy and unfulfilled, unable to achieve enduring intimacy. And more troubling is the fact that this is not just a problem affecting the unbelieving world; it is equally a serious problem affecting the Body of Christ. Our local churches today are filled with people who are sadly unhappy and unfulfilled in their marriages.

The fundamental reason for this unfortunate condition may be a lack of clear understanding of the origin of marriage or a blatant disregard for or rejection of God's plan and purpose for marriage.

In our generation, the essence of marriage has been reduced to a matter of personal view and opinion. There are those today who are trying to redefine marriage to fit their own lifestyles. And there are those who seem to view marriage as uncertain and unstable. Hence, the younger generation of our day is in a state of dilemma and confusion as to the importance and significance of marriage as ordained by God.

Every living and breathing society is founded on the strength of the family unit. Thus, when the family unit is broken down or becomes dysfunctional, the larger society will obviously be thrown into a state of chaos and instability. The problems facing our world today, teen pregnancies, violence, the wanton abuse of human life through the evil of abortion, the worship and adoration of immorality and other vices, are largely due to the breakdown of the traditional family. The institution of marriage created and ordained by God has undoubtedly become the victim of a reckless and dubious society, a society that seems to have lost every sense of right and wrong.

Apart from a lack of clear knowledge of God's plan and intention for marriage, the rejection of God's definition and value of marriage is another deadly problem that is gradually eating deep into the very fabric of our contemporary marital unions. Marriage from God's perspective, in the simplest terms, may be described as the union between a man and a woman with the promise of sharing their lives together in a covenantal lifelong relationship until death parts them. And when they are blessed with children, both the man and the woman are called upon to nurture and train them in the way of the Lord. Unfortunately, the world is desperately trying to formulate new definitions and standards for marriage and family.

It is obvious that the more we try to do it our own way, the more compounded marital crises have become. The rate at which marriages are broken down today is very alarming. And sadly enough, the ghost of divorce is not only destroying and destabilizing our contemporary world, it is gradually disrobing the Church of her moral and spiritual integrity regarding God's ordained permanent state of marriage. The rate of divorce today is no different within the Body of Christ than it is for people of the world.

If we are going to experience fulfillment and stability as intended by God in our marital relationships, we must return to God, the author of marriage and family. We must accept God's plan as the only constant and sure standard for lasting and enduring marital union. The issue of marriage and family cannot and must not be allowed to be governed by the weak and unstable passion and opinion of fallible man, but by the divine and perfect wisdom of the Almighty God, revealed and given to us in His unfailing word. Thus, every man or woman desiring to enter into this most intimate relationship possible among humankind must be able to say, "Lord, thy will be done."

This book is written with the following convictions that:

1. God is the author of marriage and family (Genesis 2:15-25).

2. God intended marriage to be satisfying and fulfilling (Proverbs 5:18-19).

3. God intended marriage to be permanent (Mark 10:5-9; Matthew 19:3-9; Malachi 2:16; 1 Corinthians 7:10).

4. God intended marriage to be a covenantal relationship between a man and a woman (Genesis 1:27-27; Malachi 2:14-15; Proverbs 2:17; Matthew 19:4-6; Mark 10:7).

5. Both the man and the woman share equal dignity before God, and they were both made to complement each other in a companionship relationship (Genesis 1:27-28; 1 Peter 3:7).

6. Marriage and family can be joyful and exciting (Psalm 28).

7. The marriage institution as ordained by God is the bedrock of a living and vibrant society (Genesis 1:27-28).

8. Marriage is an exclusive relationship (Exodus 20:14; Proverbs 5:15; Matthew 5:27-28).

9. God intended the marriage bed to be kept holy (Hebrews 13:4).

10. God can breathe life into a dying marital union, if the wives and husbands in these relationships are

willing to surrender all to God at the foot of the cross (Psalm 30:5; Jeremiah 31:13; Isaiah 40:31).

This book in part, is a product some of my doctoral research papers and project presented to the faculty of Golden Gate Baptist Theological Seminary, Mill Valley, California. In this regard, I wish to express my profound thanks to all the seminary faculty, particularly my advisors, Professors Leroy Gainey and Dwight A. Honeycutt, for their affirmations and invaluable suggestions. Above all, I give God all the glory for the possibility of writing this book. My earnest prayer is that God will use it to breathe freshness and wholeness into marriages.

This book is divided into four chapters. The first chapter deals with the theological rationale for equal companionship relationships that should exist in a vibrant Christian marital union. The second chapter examines what I have called the "Ten Commandments" of marriage. The third chapter deals with the deceptive substitutes for marital relationships, and the fourth chapter examines the fundamentals of interpersonal relationships as they relate to martial union. I am persuaded that anyone seeking the will of God in marriage as ordained by God will find this book uplifting and insightful. It is my prayer that this book will be a blessing to many couples and those who are planning to enter this great institution of marriage, the most important relationship possible among men.

Thelogical Rationale for Equal Companionship Relationship in Marriage

That both male and female share equal worth and dignity before God.

That both male and female were made for companionship relationship.

Marriage is a divine institution created and ordained by God (Genesis 2:18-24). In other words, marriage is more than a social engagement devised by man for his own convenience; it is from God Himself, the author of marriage.[1] Pope Pius XI underscored this when he said, "Let this remain the unchanged and unmovable foundation, that matrimony is not the institution of man; nor did man restore it, it is of God."[2] Also, in Genesis 1:28, God equally commissioned both the man and woman to rule over "every living creature that moves on the ground." God created and designed the man and woman to be partners sharing the same authority, uniqueness, and dignity.[3] The creation accounts of Genesis 1 and 2 contain no hint that the woman is subordinate to man.[4] The accounts make no attempt to set the male as a superior human with the female tagging along for the benefit of the male.[5] God formed and created them to function as equal companions. He intended them to correspond to each other, to share together their thoughts, goals, plans, efforts, and bodies as equal companions. This chapter examines the case for equal companionship from three basic theological dimensions:

1. In the Image of God;
2. One Flesh; and
3. Submit to One Another.

In the Image of God

God created man in His own image, in the image of God He created him; male and female He created them (Genesis 1:27 NASB).

Man's distinctiveness is that he is created in the image of God.[6] Drawing from the creation story, the Bible affirms that humanity, both male and female, are created in the divine image of God. Their minds and their souls have in a way been formed after the nature and perfection of God; hence, they are able to cooperate with God in the continuing work of creation.[7] God created men and women equally in His image, and they share in equal dignity.[8] Indeed, the reflection of the image of God in every man and woman makes him or her valuable.[9] Therefore, since the woman is a creature of God just as man is and is made in God's image and likeness (Genesis 5:1-2), she is of equal dignity, worth, and value as man, especially as his partner in a marriage relationship.[10]

One Flesh

For this reason a man shall leave his father and his mother, and be joined to his wife; and they shall become one flesh (Genesis 2:24 NIV).

Scholars interpret the phrase "one flesh" to mean unity or oneness between married partners. Expanding on this, Herbert and Fern Miles write:

"One flesh is a total relationship of the whole person of the husband to the total person of his wife, and the whole person of the wife to the total person of her husband. One flesh affects the whole self of both husband and wife. So, "to become one flesh" carries with it the fullness of fellowship in a companionship relationship."[12]

Husband and wife becoming one flesh cannot be adequately achieved if the wife is still being looked upon as a subordinate of her husband because of her gender difference. Along this line, Herbert and Fern Miles further argue that "the one-flesh unity is in direct conflict with the dominant/subordinate concept."[13] For one flesh can only become more meaningful when a Christian husband and wife are mutually connected in all areas affecting their relationship.

Becoming one flesh involves more than sexual relations or physical union; it is the total giving of oneself to another person in a companionship relationship.[14] To this issue of one flesh, Wayne Mack writes:

> *"One flesh concept must manifest itself in practical, tangible, demonstrable ways. God does not intend it to be merely an abstract concept or idealistic theory, but a concise reality. Total intimacy and deep unity are part of God's blueprint for a good marriage."*[15]

Therefore, to achieve total intimacy, deep unity, and oneness within the context of the one-flesh principle, we must understand the character of marriage.

The Permanent Character of Marriage

Marriage is intended by God to be a permanent relationship. By its very nature, it is a divine institution, a uniting of personalities, and a permanent relationship.[16] In keeping with the relationship principle in Mark 10:9 and Matthew 19:6 that *"what therefore God hath joined together, let no man put asunder"* (KJV), we must come to a firm conviction that God's ideal and intent for marriage is that marriage be permanent and indissoluble.[17] According to Karl Barth, "when marriage is seen in the light of the divine command then it is clear that it is a lasting life partnership."[18] And furthermore, Karl Barth maintained that "to enter upon marriage is to renounce the possibility of leaving it."[19]

Jesus made it abundantly clear when He was asked

whether it was lawful for a man to divorce his wife (Matthew 19:3) that from the beginning, God intended the institution of marriage to be a life-long relationship. This being true, it follows that we cannot fully know, understand, and experience the permanent nature of marriage until we see marriage as a partnership between a man and a woman of equal worth and value before God.[20] God has uniquely given marriage as the most meaningful and fulfilling model of companionship possible among humans.[21]

The Covenant Character of Marriage

Christian marriage is a covenantal union. It is a relationship bound by steadfast love, faithfulness, and devotion.[22] The word *covenant* may be translated as "a binding pact" in the Old Testament or "a unilateral agreement" in the New Testament, in which God dictated all terms.[23]

The Bible student may classify the biblical concept of covenant into two categories: 1) the covenant between God and human, and 2) the covenant between human and human. From biblical history, God has related to people through divine-human covenants from beyond the formation of the people of Israel to the new covenant sealed with the death and resurrection of Jesus Christ.[24] Moreover, the relationships between Ruth and Naomi and David and Jonathan are good examples of human-to-human covenant relationships filled with love, trust, and loyalty.[25] Both categories of covenant clearly demonstrate that a covenant is not just a public promise we make, but a commitment to act lovingly and loyally no matter what the cost.[26]

Covenant love and care for each other in marriage relationships mirror God's love and care for us.[27] Love, not power, and responsibilities, not rights, direct the relationship between covenant partners in marriage.[28]

Male domination is destructive to the oneness of covenant marriage. Covenant marriage, if it is to be happy, meaningful, and harmonious, must develop around husband–wife roles that are truly complementary and individually satisfying.[29] Neither spouse is to assign the other an inferior status nor make him or her subject to the dominating control of the other.[30]

Submit to One Another

Several biblical scholars have consistently used the word *submit* to describe the role of wives to their husbands. They usually begin their discussion with verse 22 of Ephesians chapter 5. This is not hard to understand since most translations begin a new paragraph or sentence with 22.[31]

In the Greek text, the word *submit* does not appear in verse 22, for that verse is a subordinate clause without a verb.[32] The translators have added the verb from verse 21, which is translated, "Submit to one another out of reverence for Christ."[33] Grammatically, verses 21 and 22 ought to have been treated as one verse. It is a call for mutual submission among Christians in their relationships. Mutual submission is therefore a significant key in a Christian marriage. Husbands and wives are to submit to one another in their relationships out of reverence for Christ. For mutual submission to be meaningful, it must grow out of equal companionship. Christian couples must relate to one another as companions, and they can then experience the joy of mutual submission.

However, while we need to understand marriage in terms of mutual submission, we must also understand God-given roles in marriage. It is clear in scriptures that the man has been assigned the role of headship in marriage within the context of the administration of family affairs. The word of God says, *"For the husband is the head of the wife as Christ is the head of the church, his body, of which he is the Savior. Now as the church submits to Christ, so also wives should submit to their husbands in everything"* (Ephesians 5:23-24). This is not subordination as the system of the world would make us believe; this is a voluntary submission of the wife to the leadership of her husband. God is the God of order and not confusion. So He has given to man the principle of family administration so that orderliness may prevail within the society. For example, two presidents cannot rule a nation at the same time; neither can two principals govern a school at the same time. Therefore, the voluntary submission of the wife to her husband's leadership is vital to the welfare of the family. It is God's specific instruction to the wife regarding her role in the administration of marriage and family (1 Peter 3:1-2), as the husband was also instructed specifically to love his wife as Christ loves the Church (Ephesians 5:25).

Obviously the ship of the family cannot be steered by two captains or else the ship will sink. Indeed, this submission is not in contradiction to the mutual submission that both husband and wife must share out of reference for Christ.

As we end this chapter, let us try to examine some relational principles as they relate to the fundamental issue of oneness and mutual submission in a companionship marriage.

A Description of Christian Marriage

Christian marriage is a relationship in which a man and a woman who love each other share a common dream and spend their lives making the dream come true.[34] Christian marriage is the merging of two persons, their bodies, emotions, minds, and souls—the blending of the streams of two lives into one current.[35] It is the coming together of two people, a man and a woman, with the promise of sharing each other's joys, goods, and sorrows.

From the spiritual standpoint, marriage has a very deep spiritual significance. Christian marriage not only sees men and women as physical, but also spiritual; therefore, marriage unites two people into one body and one spirit.[36] The New Testament uses marriage as a symbol of the relationship between Christ and the Church.[37]

Made for Companionship: A Significant Purpose of Christian Marriage

"It is not good for the man to be alone" (Genesis 2:18). These words precisely reflect God's sensitivity to man's need of human companionship.[38] God had provided the other creatures with companions of their own kind, but Adam was alone—no one could understand his needs or share his responsibilities.[39] Hence, God created Eve and introduced her to Adam; He wanted them to have fellowship, to have each other's companionship, and to live for the other, and both were to live for God.[40] It is indeed proper to say that one of the significant purposes of marriage is that men and women in marriage relationships are made to provide companionship for one another. God has made them to share their lives together as equal companions. Hence, sexual fulfillment, bearing and guiding of children, and providing an environment for spiritual growth can be exciting and uplifting when married partners understand equal companionship as an important factor in marriage.

Wholesome Sexual Fulfillment and Procreation

The husband should fulfill his marital duty to his wife, and likewise the wife to her husband. The wife's body does not belong to her alone but also to her husband. In the same way, the husband's body does not belong to him alone but also to his wife (1 Corinthians 7:3-4).

Sexual drive is a significant part of human nature created by God. God created man and woman as sexual beings: *"...male and female he created them"* (Genesis 1:27). He invited the man and woman to participate with Him in the propagation of the human race. *"Be fruitful and increase in number"* (Genesis 1:28). Stephen Grunlan concurs: "Sex in marriage is God sanctioned and God ordained. It is a physical bonding between a husband and wife."[41] According to Paul's injunction in 1 Corinthians 7:3-4, husband and wife are to share mutual responsibility for the sexual fulfillment of one another. Sexual union and the blessing of procreation involve the wholeness of the man and woman: the mind (*nous*), soul (*psyche*), body (*soma*), spirit (*pneuma*), and the heart (*kardia*).

In a Christian marriage, sexual experiences can be a sustaining and rewarding expression of oneness and wholeness when entered into with the freedom of self-giving and respect for one another.[42] Mutual respect and submission in partnership marriage provides an avenue for wholesome sexual fulfillment. In the one-flesh relationship (Genesis 2:24), husband and wife belong to each other in unity and wholeness.

Sexual relations are to be equal and reciprocal.[43] Marriage partners must honor the uniqueness of each other in order to experience sexual fulfillment as intended by God.

End Notes

[1] Charles Kindregan, *A Theology of Marriage: A Doctrinal, Moral and Legal Study* (Milwaukee: The Bruce Publishing Company, 1967), 12.

[2] Kindregan, *A Theology of Marriage,* 12, citing Pope Pius XI, Casti Connubii, A.A.S. 22 (1930).

[3] Vernon O. Elmore, *Layman's Library of Christian Doctrine: Man as God's Creation* (Nashville: Broadman Press, 1986), 110.

[4] John C. Howell, *Equality and Submission in Marriage* (Nashville: Broadman Press, 1979), 38.

[5] Elmore, *Man as God's Creation,* 110.

[6] William L. Hendricks, *The Doctrine of Man* (Nashville: Convention Press, 1977), 53.

[7] Clarke Adams, *The Holy Bible Containing the Old and New Testaments: A Commentary and Critical Notes, vol. 1, Genesis to Deuteronomy* (New York: Abingdon Press, n.d.), 38.

[8] Elmore, *Man as God's Creation,* 110.

[9] Hendricks, *The Doctrine of Man,* 52.

[10] Joseph O.S.C. Fichtner, *Man the Image of God* (New York: Alba House, 1978), 42.

[11] Herbert J. Miles and Fern H. Miles, *Husband-Wife Equality* (Old Tappan, NJ: Fleming H. Revell Co., 1978), 165.

[12] Geoffrey W. Bromiley, *God and Marriage* (Grand Rapids: Williams B. Eerdmans Publishing Company, 1980), 3.

[13] Miles and Miles, *Husband-Wife Equality,* 165.

14 Wayne Mack, *Strengthening Your Marriage* (Phillipsburg, New Jersey: Presbyterian and Reformed Publishing Co., 1977), 4.

15 Ibid., 4.

16 Charles Edward Smith, *Commitment: The Cement of Love* (Nashville: Broadman Press, 1982), 36.

17 Ibid., 33.

18 Karl Barth, *On Marriage* (Philadelphia: Fortress Press, 1968), 29.

19 Ibid., 29.

20 Smith, *Commitment,* 31.

21 Ibid., 36.

22 Jimmy Hester et al. eds., *Covenant Marriage* (Nashville: The Sunday School Board of the Southern Baptist Convention, 1987), 14.

23 William H. Gentz et al. eds. *The Dictionary of Bible and Religion* (Nashville: Abingdon Press, 1986), 229.

24 Hester, *Covenant Marriage,* 14.

25 Ibid.

26 Ibid.

27 Ibid.

28 Ibid.

29 Dwight Hervey Small, *Marriage As Equal Partnership* (Grand Rapids: Baker Book House, 1980), 16.

30 Ibid.

31 Stephen A. Grunlan, *Marriage and the Family* (Grand Rapids, Michigan: Zondervan Publishing House, 1984), 147.

32 Ibid.

33 Ibid.

[34] Cliff Allbritton, *How to Get Married and Stay That Way* (Nashville: Broadman Press, 1982), 7-8.

[35] Ibid.

[36] Kamua Wa Githumbi et al., *Marriage Before and After* (Achimota, Ahana: African Christian Press, 1982), 76-77.

[37] Ibid.

[38] Elmore, *Man as God's Creation*, 111.

[39] Ibid, 111.

[40] Githumbi, *Marriage Before and After,* 3.

[41] Grunlan, *Marriage and the Family,* 156.

[42] Howell, *Christian Marriage: Growing in Oneness,* 35.

[43] Ed Wheat and Gloria Okes Perkins, *The First Years of Forever* (Grand Rapids: Zondervan Publishing House, 1988), 88.

2

Ten Commandments of Marriage

On Mount Sinai, God gave to the nation of Israel ten "decalogues" or commandments through Moses, to guide and to preserve the integrity of Israel as God's treasured possession. Along the same lines, the ten commandments of marriage presented in this chapter are basic guidelines from God's word, designed to guide and preserve the sanctity and integrity of marriage and family as ordained by God. It is also a suggested set of guidelines to help produce an enduring marital union to the glory of God. These ten commandments are put forth as covenants of blessings, designed to bless and edify the divine institution of marriage.

First Commandment

Thou shalt love the LORD thy God with all thine heart, and with all thy soul, and with all thy might (Deuteronomy 6:5 KJV).

Marriage is undoubtedly a unique relationship created and ordained by God. It is probably the most complex relationship on the face of the earth. Because of its complexities, people are warned not to enter it without due consideration. God Almighty is the creator of the earth (Genesis 1:1-2). When the whole world has ceased to exist, God will still be God. He is not only the origin and beginning of the universe; He is the creator and author of the institution of marriage. Hence, for marriage partners to experience a happy and fulfilling marital union as intended by God, both partners must establish a personal relationship with the Lord of the institution of marriage. The admonition of God to Israel as a chosen nation is very clear: *"Hear O Israel: The LORD our God, the LORD is one. Love the Lord your God with all your heart and with all your soul and with all your strength"* (Deuteronomy 6:4-5). God demands Israel's total loyalty and devotion to Him; He demands the first place in the heart and soul of Israel as a nation. The same God then is the same God today, and He demands no less. Thus, in our church age, if anyone desires to enter into a covenantal relationship with God, he or she must come with undivided heart and commitment through the atoning sacrifice of the Lord Jesus Christ on the cross of Calvary.

Our relationship with the Almighty God through our Lord and Savior Jesus Christ calls for the same intensity of devotion and loyalty because it forms the foundation of our other relationships. According to Ernest White, the author of *The Art of Human Relations*, we live and move and have our being in relationships, the most important of which is our relationship with God. It determines the quality of our marital union. It is when we love God with all of our heart and with all of our soul and with all of our strength that we can truly love our mates with the love of God and experience a joyful and enduring marital union.

Loving God with all of your heart, with all of your soul, and with all of your strength demands:

* That you accept His saving grace in Christ Jesus;
* That you deny yourself and take up your cross daily and follow Him;
* That you seek God first in all the affairs of your life;
* That you recognize God Almighty as the Alpha and Omega in every step that you take;
* That you remain totally reliant on God's leadership and providential care; and
* That you remain undivided in your loyalty, obedience, and commitment to God and His divine will, because your relationship with Him will help define the quality of your marital relationship.

Indeed, if we are not having a good relationship with God in our Christian walk, it will undoubtedly affect other areas of our interpersonal relationships. If we are going to maintain healthy marital relationships, we must maintain a true and genuine relationship with the Lord. We must surrender all and live a holy and righteous life in our Christian walk. In Paul's words of exhortation to the Colossians, he encouraged them to walk in a manner worthy of the Lord, to please God in all respects, to bear fruit in every good work, and to increase in the knowledge of God (Colossians 1:1-10).

Our sense of being and worth is derived from our relationship with God, and it is through this relationship that we can better relate in our relationship with God, and it is through *this* relationship that we can better relate in our marital relationships. Our relationships with our wives or husbands will become meaningful and uplifting when they flow from our relationship with our Lord and Savior Jesus Christ, who willingly laid down His life for us (John 15:13). Jesus, in His call for deep or intimate relationships, said, *"I am the vine; you are the branches. If a man remains in me and I in him, he will bear much fruit; apart from me you can do nothing"* (John 15:5). Our commitment and devotion to the Lord will empower us to be committed, devoted, and faithful in our marriages. Truly, our relationship with God through our Lord Jesus is the first priority. It is the foundation on which a healthy marital union is built.

Second Commandment

Thou shall acknowledge and make God the architect of thy marriage: *"Unless the LORD builds the house, its builders labor in vain. Unless the LORD watches over the city, the watchmen stand guard in vain"* (Psalm 127:1).

An *architect* is described in the *New Webster's Dictionary* as a person whose profession is to design buildings or structures and to see that his plans are correctly followed by the builders. By accepting God's saving grace, you are accepting His plan and purpose as the divine architect of your life, which includes your marital life. Thus, when you allow God to be the architect, the designer, the foundation, and the builder of your marriage, you will experience a joyful and peaceful marital union. The Psalmist clearly says that, *"Unless the LORD builds the house, they labor in vain who build it"* (Psalm 127:1 NASB). In other words, unless we allow God to be the designer and builder of our home in terms of marital union, we labor in vain if we try to do it on our own.

The prophet Jeremiah recognized the significance of God's sovereign rule over the affairs of human life when he said in chapter 10:23, *"I know, O LORD, that a man's life is not his own; it is not for man to direct his steps."* Paul, writing to the Corinthian Christians in 2 Corinthians 3:5, said, *"Not that we are competent in ourselves to claim anything for ourselves, but our competence comes from God."* And, moreover, the writer of the Book of Proverbs also said in chapter 3:6, *"In all your ways acknowledge him and he will make your paths straight."* All these selected verses speak of one thing: complete dependence and reliance on God in all your ways. He is not only the designer, He is also the builder of the totality of your life. When He is allowed to direct your steps, He will lead you in making the right choice of marriage partner. Trusting in your own wisdom or knowledge will lead to pain and sorrow. You see, our competence is found not in the weakness of human abilities but in the competence of God.

Making God the architect of your marriage means accepting God's plan and purpose in your desire to enter the divine institution of marriage. It means God alone is allowed to govern, design, and build the union, which includes the choice of partner, the celebration of communion, and the life-long process of matrimony. It reaffirms God's claim of ownership upon your life and on all your endeavors and relationships, which includes the divine union of marriage. It is the acceptance of God's will in your marital union.

When God through the risen Lord, Jesus Christ, is allowed to be the architect, designer, and builder of your marriage, your marital life will be filled with the comfort and peace of God that transcends all human understanding. This is not to say you will not experience some moments of conflict in your relationship, but when you do, you can always seek the guidance of the one who is the architect of your life and marriage through the Holy Scripture. The word of God says:

> Do not be anxious about anything, but in everything, by prayer and petition, with thanksgiving, present your request to God. And the peace of God, which transcends all understanding, will guard your hearts and your minds in Christ Jesus (Philippians 4:6-7).

The "peace" stipulated in this passage does not in any way suggest an absence of conflict. But it is a peace that reigns in the heart and soul of a child of God even in the midst of a problematic situation. It is a God-given peace that enables Christian couples to walk victoriously through difficult days.

Third Commandment

Thou shall love each other with a self-giving, sacrificial love: *"Love is patient, love is kind. It does not envy, it does not boast, it is not proud. It is not rude, it is not self-seeking"* (1 Corinthians 13:4-5).

Since the dawn of time, man has struggled in the weakness of his mind to define and interpret what love is. Love has been merely described as feeling. That is why many people fall in love and immediately fall out of love when the feelings are gone. Love has also been misinterpreted to mean what individuals can get out of it rather than the giving of self to another person. Thus, human definitions of love based on human values and traditions are inadequate to sustain a meaningful and lasting marital relationship.

Moreover, I believe it is because of the limitation of human understanding of biblical love that some people, even the so-called Christian scholars, have come to the tragic conclusion that "love is not enough" in the sustenance of marriage. I believe if they are referring to the human view or definition of love, yes, this kind of love is not enough because it is inadequate and insufficient to sustain a marital union. But if they are saying "biblical love" is not enough, I would say with all humility that they are wrong. I am convinced and persuaded that God's kind of love, as revealed in His unfailing word, is strong enough when genuinely implemented to sustain any marriage.

All other aspects of marital relationships—financial responsibilities, communication, appreciation, and so on—rest firmly on this biblical love. Many marriages are in shambles today because they are founded on counterfeit love. Marriage is God's idea. He created it and ordained it. And He gave us an instructional guide, the Bible. And in it we are abundantly instructed on the kind of love that can sustain marital union. In the New Testament we see three expressions of love: *eros* (the feeling love), *philia* (the friendship love), and *agape* (the self-giving, unconditional love). In his instructional guide, God expects every believer to move beyond eros and philios into a higher plane of love: the sacrificial, unconditional love (agape). When agape love forms the foundation of a marital union, there will be contentment, fulfillment, and satisfaction. This kind of love does not mean there will be an absence of conflict or life's storms, but it is a kind of love that is able to enrich, rekindle, empower, and sustain marital unions even in the midst of the storms of life.

Agape love (sacrificial and self-giving, John 3:16; 1 Corinthians 13):

* Is not based on mere feelings; it is a responsibility.

* Is not based on performance; it is self-giving.

* Is not based on the status of the man or the woman, it is based on the worth and value of the man or woman as God's creation.

* Is not based merely on appearance; it is the inner beauty and devotion to the Lord. The Bible says, *"Charm is deceptive, and beauty is fleeting; but a woman who fears the LORD is to be praised"* (Proverbs 31:30).

* Is not based on probability; it rests upon the principle of permanency—until death do us part.

* Is a choice. *"For God so loved the world that he gave his one and only Son, that whoever believes in him shall not perish but have eternal life"* (John 3:16). God Almighty in His sovereign rule chose to love us and to give Himself for us in his one and only Son Jesus Christ, for the redemption of our souls. This choice is a personal act of compassion and commitment. So loving God and others particularly in marriage is a choice.

* Is self-giving. It is the giving of your self 100 per cent to another person in a holy matrimony. It causes you to want to meet the needs of your husband or wife instead of being self-seeking or self-centered. Imagine two people in a marital union who are self-giving, looking for the good of one another; they both will experience a joyful relationship.

In 1 Corinthians 13:4-7, God gave us a vivid picture of His kind of love:

Love is patient, love is kind. It does not envy, it does not boast, it is not proud. It is not rude, it is not self-seeking, it is not easily angered, it keeps no record of wrongs. Love does not delight in evil but rejoices with the truth. It always protects, always trusts, always hopes, always perseveres.

God's word made it emphatically clear that this kind of love can never fail (1 Corinthians 13:8). Many waters cannot quench this love (Song of Songs 8:7). Rivers of pain, hurts, conflicts, or some other problems may try to quench this love or drown it, but they cannot because it is deeply rooted in who God is, for God Himself is Love (1 John 4:16). When a husband and a wife choose to love each other, with the love of God they are destined to enjoy a lasting and enduring marital union.

Fourth Commandment

Thou shall have and maintain a family altar: *"Let us then approach the throne of grace with confidence, so that we may receive mercy and find grace to help us in our time of need"* (Hebrews 4:16).

The family altar is a unique time set apart for family worship. It is a place where the family gathers together to sing praise songs, read God's word, and pray. It is a moment that enables the couple to share their faith with each other and their children. It is at the family alter that Christian couples continue to celebrate the praise and adoration of God and continue to renew and reaffirm their relationship with God and each other. It is where they will continually find grace to help them in times of conflict and difficulties, for the word of God admonishes believers to "*...come boldly to the throne of grace, that we may obtain mercy and find grace to help in time of need*" (Hebrews 4:16 NKJV). At the Christian altar, burdens are lifted and Christian marriage partners learn to cast all their cares upon the Lord (1 Peter 5:7). Couples will continue to renew their strength: when the storms of life come raging, "*...they shall mount up with wings as eagles; they shall run, and not be weary; and they shall walk, and not faint*" (Isaiah 40:31 KJV). It is at the family alter that Christian couples celebrate their commitment and devotion to one another and where their children learn obedience and the fear of the Lord.

Fifth Commandment

Thou shall not defile the marriage bed. Marriage should be honored by all, and the marriage bed kept pure, for God will judge the adulterer and all the sexually immoral (Hebrews 13:4).

In Genesis 2:25 we see the following binding concepts in the marital union:

Leaving: a picture of maturity and autonomy.

Cleaving: a picture of the man being united only to his wife.

One-flesh principle: the man becoming one flesh only with his wife.

First, the defilement of the marriage bed in holy matrimony is a sin against God and your body. The Bible says those who sow to please the sinful desires of the flesh, which includes adultery, will reap corruption. Moreover, the body of a believer is a living temple of God. And whatever you do with your body must bring honor and glory to God. For God Almighty will surely judge the adulterer. Second, the defilement of the marriage bed destroys the oneness in the marital union. The oneness in marriage is God's design and intention. Thus, to defile the marriage bed is to profane the oneness divinely instituted by God in marital union. And third, the defilement of the marriage bed destroys the trust that binds the relationship together; it is a flagrant abuse and violation of marital vows. In interpersonal relationships, trust takes time and effort to build. Thus, when the trust in a marital relationship is violated, it is always hazardous to the health of the union. That is why couples must strive to nurture the trust principle in their relationship. Without trust, it would be hard for a marriage partner to have a meaningful and fulfilling marital union as intended by God. The marriage bed must be kept pure and holy—that is the will and command of God. Any violation of this will of God, particularly by a child of God, will be seen as a reckless act of disobedience against God.

Sixth Commandment

Thou shall keep no record of wrongs. *"Love is patient, love is kind. It does not envy, it does not boast…it keeps no record of wrongs"* (1 Corinthians 13:4-5).

A couple once came to a pastor for counseling because of their seemingly unending quarreling, disputes, and everyday growling at each other. After a preliminary session with the pastor, the pastor gave the couple an assignment. A box was given to each of the spouses. For a week, instead of growling at each other, the pastor instructed them to write every wrong done to them by their spouse each time it occurred and put it in their individual box. They were instructed to return to his office after a week for another counseling session. Thus, after the one-week assignment, the couple returned to the pastor's office with the boxes. When the boxes were opened, the wife's box was filled with many wrongs done to her by her husband: when he left his shoes in the living room; when he failed to take out the trash on time because he was reading the newspaper; when she had to walk the children to school because her husband forgot to take the car out for a tune up. However, when the husband's box was opened only one thing was found: "I love you no matter what."

Keeping a record of wrongs in a conflict situation is not the answer. Conflict itself is not evil, it all depends on how the couple handles it. When conflict occurs, some couples may choose to use inappropriate methods to deal with the conflict. For example:

* Avoidance or withdrawal: not willing to talk about the problem.

* My way: this is an insistence on one's stand that "you are wrong, I am right." This is a selfish, self-centered attitude.

* Give in: an attitude of "I am wrong, you are right"—trying to avoid quarrel or confrontation without a healthy resolution of the conflict.

Conflict resolution should be based on the following principles:

* A mutual understanding of what the problem is.

* An honest and mutual analysis of the problem.

* From the spirit of humility and meekness, couples should not be ashamed to acknowledge fault.

* Christian couples should learn to forgive each other. The joy of being forgiven and being able to forgive others cannot be overemphasized. It is a mark of a true believer.

* Resolution of conflict may also call for compromise.

* When an issue has been resolved, couples should close that chapter and should let it remain closed. By following this basic principle couples will turn conflict into blessings.

Keeping a record of wrongs will only lead to weariness and heaviness of heart.

Seventh Commandment

Thou shall continually celebrate your love for one another appreciating the uniqueness of each other.

> *How delightful is your love, my sister, my bride! How much more pleasing is your love than wine and fragrance of your perfume than any spice! Your lips drop sweetness as the honeycomb, my bride; milk and honey are under your tongue. The fragrance of your garments is like that of Lebanon...You are a garden fountain, a well of flowing water* (Song of Songs 4:10-15).

The word *celebration* means to praise, to honor, or to keep holy. The people of Israel were commanded by God to celebrate annually certain events in commemoration or remembrance of their significance in Israel's history. Some of these unique events are recorded in Leviticus 23: the Sabbath Day, the Feast of the Passover and Unleavened Bread; the Day of Atonement, the Feast of the Tabernacles, and others. As believers in the Lord Jesus Christ, we are called upon to daily celebrate the goodness of God. As a body of Christ, we come together every Sunday and at other times to praise and to honor the Lord our God. This act of solemn worship in our celebration of God's grace and goodness regularly refreshes our love and commitment toward Him.

In like manner, couples should learn to appreciate the uniqueness of one another in the celebration of love for each other. In the process of celebration, couples must daily cherish and appreciate one another:

1. By treating each other with respect, honor, affection, and tender care. One woman was quoted as saying, "The most wonderful part of being married is going to sleep every night on my husband's shoulder with his arm around me. I feel so safe and loved."

2. By expressing your love in tangible ways, like a surprise gift to your spouse to show your appreciation for him or her. The gift does not have to be expensive; it is the thoughtfulness that your partner will appreciate.

3. By paying attention to one another and not to TV, the newspaper, or other objects of distraction.

4. By spending quality time together, maybe going out on a date or planning a vacation together. When couples fail to celebrate their marital union, the union will become dull and uninteresting.

When couples make an effort in their love for each other to regularly praise and honor their union, their love for each other will be strengthened and rekindled; their passion for each other will be refreshed and their commitment and devotion to one another will be renewed. Furthermore, when couples regularly appreciate one another, it will continually breathe life into their marital relationship and will also empower and strengthen their affection for each other and their total union.

When couples make it a joyful habit to celebrate their marital relationship, even though the physical body may be wearing out, their love for each other will be forever young and vibrant.

Eighth Commandment

Thou shall manage faithfully the financial resources God has given to you. *"The earth is the LORD's, and everything in it, the world, and all who live in it"* (Psalm 24:1). *"Now it is required that those who have been given a trust must prove faithful"* (1 Corinthians 4:2).

The joy of sharing and working together in marriage includes responsible financial management. The issue of finance in marriage can be very troublesome and unpleasant. No subject is as divisive and explosive as the issue of finance in interpersonal relationships, particularly in marital union. Because marriage is a total union and a total commitment between two people who care for each other, the issue of finance must be handled properly according to God's plan, because if it is not handled properly, it may destroy marital trust, happiness, and unity.

The following are some basic guidelines for effective financial management God's way.

A. Background for Managing Financial Resources God's Way

The Bible tells us that *"the earth is the LORD's, and everything in it, the world, and all who live in it"* (Psalm 24:1). If marriage partners are going to experience joy and harmony in the way they manage their God-given financial resources, they both must be willing to do it God's way.

51

God owns all that He has created. The world and everything in it belongs to Him including you, your spouse, your children. and everything you have (1 Chronicles 19:11,14).

God Almighty is the one who gives you health and vitality of life that enables you to work and make money (Deuteronomy 8:18).

You are a steward of what you have, and you and your spouse are called upon to be faithful stewards of all that God has provided and given to you. The parable of the talents illustrates for us this Biblical stewardship principle (Matthew 25:14-30).

He owns all that we have, including that which remains after the tithe is given. Stewardship involves all of life (Romans 14:8).

A Christian who is considering marriage needs to understand the other person's view regarding money because the religious belief of one person about money may be different from the other person. This is one more reason why a Christian should not be yoked together with an unbeliever (2 Corinthians 6:14).

Furthermore, Christian partners considering marriage should discuss with each other their assets and liabilities. Assets are all the possessions and money that a person owns, and liabilities are all the debts and bills an individual has. Marriage partners are entitled to know what debts they are taking on when they marry and what money is available for the partners.[1]

B. Some Financial Management Dynamics

Couples should mutually work to build their financial goals.

Both partners should participate in the financial decisions affecting their relationship.

Money is neither good nor bad in itself; an unhealthy attitude about it can be destructive (1 Timothy 6:10).

Money should be viewed as "family money," not "my money" or "your money." *"Therefore what God has joined together, let man not separate"* (Matthew 19:6).

The amount of money is not as important as how it is managed.

Use credit wisely.

Financial policies should be agreed upon by both partners and honored.

Develop a financial plan or budget acceptable to both partners using the following guidelines:

* Make the plan realistic.
* Estimate your income.
* Estimate your tithe.
* Estimate your fixed expenditures (rent, food, utilities, etc).
* Establish an emergency fund.
* Estimate your credit and loan bills.
* Each partner should be given some money without having to account for it.
* Other needs: insurance, clothing, vacation, etc.

* Estimate your savings amount.
* Avoid spending more than your net income (1 Timothy 6:6,9).

By being faithful in the management of God's money entrusted into your hands as couples, you will experience peace of mind. You will find yourself relieved from the unnecessary burden of debt.

Ninth Commandment

Thou shall cultivate and maintain a healthy system of communication. *"The Sovereign LORD has given me an instructed tongue, to know the word that sustains the weary. He wakens me morning by morning, wakens my ear to listen like one being taught"* (Isaiah 50:4).

A woman discussing her marriage with a marriage counselor was quoted as saying, "When I got married I was looking for an ideal, then it became an ordeal, and now I want a new deal."

The ability to communicate is a gift from God. God Almighty gave mankind the ability to communicate through the gift of words and many other nonverbal expressions. Through this gift we are able to send and receive messages. Communication is indeed an essential part of human life. As we relate with one another in interpersonal relationships, we are constantly communicating, sending out and receiving messages. I cannot imagine life without communication dynamics.

Because of the significance of communication to life and more so to human relationships, individual persons within the human family—and in a more unique sense, couples in marital unions—should learn how to communicate effectively. Clear and authentic communication is vital to the growth of marital relationships. It allows couples to share themselves, their feelings and emotions, to settle conflict or misunderstandings, to make decisions, to plan the family budget, and to establish shared rules and goals. A lack of good and effective communication can breed crises and make couples grow apart. Marital union can be destroyed by lack of good communication. Writing on this important issue, Preston and Genie Dyer have this to say:

> "While communication is important in every marriage, it takes on special significance in the marriage of Christians. When Christians marry, a partnership is created including the man, the woman, and God. God's understanding is complete, but the human partners must work to communicate to each other their thoughts, feelings and desires if there is to be understanding. Understanding increases the stability and strength of the partnership and helps the couples to maintain their commitments to each other and God."[2]

Couples must learn how to transmit, decode, interpret, and respond to interpersonal communication in positive and reinforcing ways.[3]

What is communication? Communication is the capacity to express or exchange thoughts, feelings, information, or the like by writing, speaking, or actions, in such a way that the other person understands what is being communicated.

Some barriers that hinder effective communication are:

* Unfaithfulness in confidential matters (Proverbs 11:13);
* A biting and cutting tongue (Proverbs 12:18);
* Lying (Proverbs 12:22);
* Thoughtless words spoken without the advantage of intellect (Proverbs 18:13); and
* A contentious spirit (Proverbs 21:19).

The following are some guidelines for effective communication:

Don't be hasty in your words. Make sure that every word spoken has been carefully considered (Proverbs 15:23,28; 21:23; 29:20).

You can disagree without quarreling (Proverbs 17:14; 20:3; Ephesians 4:31).

Put your anger under control (Proverbs 14:29; 15:1; 16:24; 25:15; Ephesians 4:26).

When you are wrong, take responsibility and say the magic words, "I am sorry" (James 5:16).

When you forgive your spouse, don't continue to bring the matter up (Colossians 3:13; Ephesians 4:32).

Avoid nagging; encourage one another (Proverbs 10:19; 17:9; Romans 12:17,21; 1 Peter 2:23; 3:9).

Learn the three methods of communication: verbal, nonverbal, and symbolic. Verbal communication involves the expression of words. Nonverbal communication is through gestures, facial expressions, and so on. Symbolic communication involves symbols, such as gifts, or cards.

Good communication skills include:

Respecting the person of your mate.

Learning to listen carefully.

Learning openness or transparency without any hidden agenda. The Bible says *"The man and his wife were both naked and they felt no shame"*—a clear symbol of complete openness (Genesis 2:25).

Learning to be truthful in words and actions (Ephesians 4:15,25; Colossians 3:9).

Clarifying nonverbal signals.

Learning to give clear and constructive feedback.

Being sure that the message heard was the message sent.

Learning to deal with issues at hand when in conflict.

Avoiding dogmatic responses like "You always…" or "I am the authority here." Instead, use inviting words such as "It seems to me…" or "Would you mind if we…."

Effective communication is a vital key to growing together in marriage. When couples learn to communicate effectively, it will empower their devotion and commitment to each other. The unity and oneness in their union will be strengthened.

Tenth Commandment

Thou shall love, nurture and train your children in the way of the Lord.

Sons are a heritage from the LORD, children a reward from him. Like arrows in the hands of a warrior are sons born in one's youth. Blessed is the man whose quiver is full of them. They will not be put to shame when they contend with their enemies in the gate (Psalm 127:3-5).

Fathers, do not exasperate your children; instead, bring them up in the training and instruction of the Lord (Ephesians 6:4).

Children are precious gifts from God; they are gracious blessings bestowed on the marital union by God. It is God's intention in marital union to continue the process of creation through human procreation. God's injunction in Genesis 1:28 concerning marital union is clear: *"Be fruitful and multiply; fill the earth"* (NKJV). Furthermore, Psalm 127:3-5 made it even clearer:

"Behold children are a heritage from the Lord, the fruit of the womb is a reward. Like arrows in the hand of a warrior, so are the children of one's youth. Happy is the man who has his quiver full of them" (NKJV).

The bearing of children is not only a blessed gift from God, it is an awesome responsibility for couples who are blessed with them. Marriage as given to us is a choice. Every individual person must make a conscious effort to enter this institution. Hence, when a couple chooses to have children, it becomes their responsibility to nurture and train the children in the way of the Lord.

Children are not intended by God to bring themselves up. God gave the parents the responsibility to *"...bring them* [children] *up in the training and admonition of the Lord* (Ephesians 6:4 KJV). The verb translated "bring up" is in the active voice, imperative mode, and present tense. It implies that children do not automatically grow up to be godly people; they have to be nurtured, disciplined, and trained in God's way. It also implies a life-long responsibility. The Bible says, *"Foolishness is bound up in the heart of a child: The rod of correction will drive it far from him"* (Proverbs 22:15 NKJV). Furthermore, the word of God made it clear that, *"The rod of correction imparts wisdom, but a child left to himself* [or herself] *disgraces his* [or her] *mother"* (Proverbs 29:15 NIV).

The following is a biblically based guideline for godly parenting:

Remember always that children are precious gifts from the Lord.

Love your child or children unconditionally.

Avoid favoring one child over another (remember the story of Joseph, Genesis 37).

Provide an environment for spiritual growth.

Diligently teach your child the word of God (Deuteronomy 6:5-7).

"Do not provoke your children to wrath." God is admonishing parents not to exasperate their children, which, according to the *New Webster's Dictionary*, means to irritate beyond measure, to make more violent or bitter, or to make rough. Your children are part of you; they are to be loved with tender care. Hence, when you reprove them, do it in love, in such a way that they are not exasperated.

Do not expect too much from what they are capable of doing (Proverbs 22:6; 1 Corinthians 13:11; Genesis 33:12-14).

Don't underestimate your children's intelligence (Romans 12:13).

Have respect for the person of your child (Proverbs 15:1; Ephesians 4:31; 1 Timothy 5:1-2). Avoid using words such as "you slob, you knuckle head, you dummy, you will never amount to anything." One man was quoted as saying that his father made a habit of calling him "dumb" or "stupid." To this day, though he is a very intelligent man with a responsible position, he still thinks of himself as dumb or stupid.[4]

Live a life of integrity before your children; practice what you preach; avoid a life of duplicity (Philippians 4:9; 1 Corinthians 11:1; Matthew 23:1-4; Deuteronomy 6:4-9).

Give room for mistakes (Colossians 3:12-14).

Teach proper values and standards (1 Peter 3:3-4; 1 Samuel 16:7).

Endeavor to spend quality time with your children (Psalm 128; Proverbs 5:15-18, Ecclesiastes 3:4).

Parents should show appreciation to their children, especially when they have done something or completed a task worthy of appreciation (1 Corinthians 13:1-8; 16:14; John 13:34-35; 1 Thessalonians 2:7-8).

Admit your mistakes to your children and ask for forgiveness when you have failed them (James 5:16; Matthew 5:23-24; Proverbs 16:2; 21:2).

Administer discipline (Proverbs 3:11-12). Discipline means to enforce learning or learning with structure:

> * Set clear boundaries (Proverbs 29:15; Exodus 20:1-17).
> * Do not give your children too many rules or rules they cannot keep (Matthew 22:34-40).
> * Do not make rules that you cannot enforce.
> * Be consistent with your discipline.
> * Be careful not to administer discipline in anger but in love (Proverbs 13:24; Revelation 3:19).
> * Explain to the child why he or she is being disciplined.

Do not allow your children to bring conflict into your relationship with your spouse.

Lift up your children in prayer always.

Couples must be united in the nurture and discipline of their children.

When parenting is done God's way, there is joy and peace in the family. It may be hard and rough; however, the future will be glorious.

End Notes

[1] Daniel G. Bagby and Michael M. Massar, *Before You Marry*, Nashville, Convention Press, 1983, p. 81

[2] Preston and Genie Dyer, *The Language of Married Love*, Nashville: Convention Press, 1988

[3] John C. Howell, Christian Marriage: Growing in Oneness, Nashville: Convention Press, 1983, p. 56

[4] Wayne Mack, *Strengthening Your Marriage* (Phillipsburg, New Jersey: Presbyterian and Reformed Publishing Co., 1977)

3

Deceptive Substitutes for Marital Relationships

Several things are working against marriage today, and this generation is in a state of dilemma because of the unstable condition of the family structure. The abandonment of God's instructional guide for marital relationship and the worship and glorification of the subtle suggestion of the evil one and the pressure of worldly teaching that stands in opposition to God are great stumbling blocks working against the stability of marital union.

The primary focus of this chapter is to present some basic substitutes influencing or affecting the institution of marriage in our generation. The word *substitute* is described in *Webster's Dictionary* as "a person or thing that takes the place of another or a word that replaces another word, phrase, or clause." Thus, the word *substitute* is used here to mean those things that have taken the place of the basic core values that have sustained marriage through the ages. It is the replacement of biblical values with worldly values and the exchange of truth for a lie. These substitutes are false and deceptive, and those who embrace them are obviously setting up themselves for a great fall. Let us now examine some of these substitutes.

Contract vs. Intimate Relationships

Marriage is often looked upon today as a contract between two people and between those two and the State,[1] rather than as an intimate relationship. I am of the opinion that this is a major problem because the word *contract* is basically a legal term based on terms and conditions devoid of feelings, emotions, and personhood. On the other hand, genuine intimacy is a process in a marriage relationship. It is a long-term combination of many strands of work and play. It is the glorious feeling of knowing a loved one's real person and of being known. It is the matchless security of knowing that someone knows us completely and still loves us.[2] Genuine intimacy builds trust. It provides a stable base for the family. It also gives roots to a relationship.[3]

Marriage relationships based on contract, making demands, setting conditions, imposing limitations, expressing doubts, seeking assurances and the like[4] without cooperative commitment is not only weak, it has no stable foundation that can withstand turbulent times. It must be noted that I am not rejecting the signing of a marriage certificate, but that marriage should not be seen as a mere contract, because to regard marriage as a contract is to equate it with a sales agreement, promissory note, job contract, or business agreement. This is one more reason why marriages are falling apart because genuine commitment is lacking.

Sentiment vs. Love

Another substitute for marriage is sentiment rather than love. Love is a concept that has been widely abused today. What many people call love today is nothing more than sentiment or infatuation. Sentiment may be described as an attitude, thought, or judgment based on feelings or emotions. Like sexual love, sentiment flickers like a candle in the wind. It blossoms and fades as the loved one succeeds and fails to deliver on the promise of fulfillment.[6] Sentiment or infatuation tends to focus on a single aspect of the other, whereas love focuses on the whole person.[7] Infatuation or sentiment is characterized by exploitation and the direct need for self-gratification.[8] Sentimental love is unstable; it is like a wave of the sea that goes up and down.

In the Bible, God's kind of love is not described in terms of feelings, but in terms of action and responsibility. Feelings are emotional reactions and the by-product of love, not the essence of love.[9] Thus, before a step as serious as marriage is considered, the two people involved need to be certain that their relationship is based on genuine love and not sentiment.[10]

Many of the so-called psychologists, marriage counselors, and even some Christian counselors and apologists of our generation have erroneously concluded that love is not enough to sustain marital union. This is because the kind of love they are talking about is not the true love of God clearly defined for us in the scriptures by Apostle Paul. This love is described for us this way:

> *Love is patient, love is kind. It does not envy, it does not boast, it is not proud. It is not rude, it is not self-seeking, it is not easily angered, it keeps no record of wrongs. Love does not delight in evil but rejoices with the truth. It always protects, always trusts, always hopes, always perseveres. Love never fails* (1 Corinthians 13:4-8).

According to God's word, this kind of love is not only enough, it never fails. *"God is love and whoever lives in love lives in God, and God in him"* (1 John 4:16). Marriage built on this kind of love will surely endure even in the midst of the inevitable storms of life.

Ceremony vs. the Celebration of Communion

Ceremony is another substitute for the celebration of communion in marital union today. Marriage from the biblical standpoint should be seen as a celebration of communion between two people who have decided to share their lives together, rather than just mere ceremony. Some people in our contemporary society see ceremony as the crowning joy of marriage; hence they are ready to spend their entire lives to make it happen.

Ceremony is good, but ceremony without communion is an empty celebration. Christian marriage is the celebration of intimate fellowship. Therefore, ceremony, even with lavish spending, without the spirit of a shared communion between the couple, is not only unfortunate, it is misguided.

The word *communion* is translated "fellowship." This fellowship has a deeper meaning in the believer's union with Christ. The word *communion* is used to describe the fellowship of the saints or believers who are in union together with a common doctrine, worship, and discipline in the Lord Jesus Christ. This communion takes a more significant meaning in Christian marriage, the highest human relationship possible on earth. This is why marriage celebration cannot be reduced to mere ceremony. The fellowship of a man and a woman in holy matrimony within the meaning of communion is based on a common faith of one Lord and one baptism. Mere ceremony in marriage without the celebration of communion is a mere ritual and formalism devoid of heavenly power and divine guidance.

Physical Attraction vs. Inner Beauty

Another substitute for marriage today is physical attraction over inner beauty. This kind of relationship is based not on anything that could properly be called love, but on a consuming drive for physical attraction and outward attributes.[11] While it is true that physical attraction is a legitimate aspect of a romantic relationship, it should not be the sole basis for a marriage.[12]

For Christians, the Bible made it abundantly clear that we should be more concerned with inner beauty than with outer beauty.[13] With the passing of years, physical attraction will fade away, but inner beauty will continue to glow.

Indeed, there is nothing wrong with finding the one whom you are considering for marriage attractive. However, physical attraction should not be seen as an end in itself, but complementary to inner beauty. Inner beauty is the total person's goals, motives, value system, lifestyle, background, character, feelings, and spiritual focus. All these put together make up the person, and not just physical attraction. Unfortunately, many people today are so overwhelmed with physical attraction that they cannot see clearly the person they are taking to the altar. For when the period of sentiment is over, they will then come face to face with the reality of marriage.

Marriage founded on the priority of physical attraction is not only founded on fantasy, but on a slippery slop of deception because "not all that glitters is gold."

Pregnancy vs. Careful Consideration

An unfortunate substitute for marriage is pregnancy. Many marriages today occur because the woman is pregnant, and the pregnancy is often far advanced before the parents discover the fact and arrange for a marriage.[14] Obviously this type of marriage was not the outcome of a careful consideration, long acquaintance, a steady growing love, an increasing recognition of the suitability of the two for each other, or their desire to merge their destinies in a lifelong companionship.[15]

Couples going into marriage should be well prepared in terms of personal understanding of lifelong commitment, financial and emotional stability, and mental and spiritual maturity. Illusion is one of the basic characteristics of marriage based on pregnancy. When the honeymoon is over, they both will come to the realization of the complexities of marriage. Since there was no good understanding of the basic rudiments of marriage, the end result may be disastrous. What, then, is going to be the fate of the child born into such a situation? Pregnancy should not in any way be seen as a substitute for a careful consideration of the person to whom one is making a life-long commitment in marriage. The decision to marry should be clearly made without any strings attached to it.

Cohabitation vs. Commitment

Another substitute for marriage is cohabitation. The institution of marriage as we know it is gradually being torn apart by our contemporary world, and cohabitation is rapidly becoming an acceptable alternative for marriage. This indeed is a very frightening situation because it poses a great danger to the stability of the institution of marriage and family.

Cohabitation is defined as "sharing a bed with someone of the opposite sex to whom one is not married."[16] According to the 1977 U.S. Census Bureau data, nearly two million unmarried couples were living together.[17] This data is indeed not representative of the world population. However, if America alone has this high figure of unmarried people living together, it is safe to say that the world population of unmarried people living together without the benefit of marriage will be very alarming and troubling.

The "deal" of cohabitation is completely open-ended—either of the partners can call it quits whenever he or she wishes. They make love, but do not make a commitment. They want more than casual sex, but less than life union.[18] What they seem to want lies somewhere between the uncertainties and anxieties of "going steady" and the certainty and commitment of marriage.[19] Between those who cohabitate, there is indeed some level of commitment, but they are unwilling to gamble on the serious or long-term commitment that marriage requires.[20] They entered something like marriage, but they do not see why a piece of legal paper filed in a clerk's office could make their partnership more meaningful, moral, or real.[21]

Live-in arrangements are tentative, transient, and temporary. They may meet a portion of the emotional needs, but because the relationship does not involve a

70

serious commitment, it usually leaves a partial emotional vacuum, instability, and scars.[22] Furthermore, children born or involved in this type of arrangement are usually emotionally deprived, if they are not ill-affected in other ways.[23]

Cohabitation has been divided into three categories: trial marriage, common-law marriage, and ad hoc arrangements.[24] No matter the category, cohabitation simply lacks the spirit of a genuine and strong commitment within the couple. Some people believe that with the high rate of divorce, it might be better for couples to live together for a while to discover if they are really compatible and would want to make the arrangement permanent.[25] However, research has shown that the rate of divorce for most couples who had cohabitated was as great as for those couples who had not. Marital satisfaction was found to be equal in both groups, but the couples who had cohabitated had more problems with alcohol, drugs, and marital infidelity.[26]

Cohabitation is against the will of God, and it breeds nothing but lawlessness, unfaithfulness, and irresponsibility.

Thus, as we look toward marriage, our focus should be on commitment rather than cohabitation. Commitment in marriage means trusting, self-giving, and being responsible. Cohabitation is not of the Lord. It is a sin in the sight of God. It condones and glorifies the sin of fornication. And no born-again child of God filled with the Holy Spirit ought to live this way.

Loneliness vs. Companionship

Some people see loneliness today as a motivation to enter into marriage. While marrying for companionship is a positive reason for marriage, marrying to avoid loneliness is a negative one.[27]

The marriage relationship is more than escaping from loneliness. It is a close, intimate relationship in which two people vowed to share their lives together. They live together, eat together, dress and undress together, sleep together, have sex together, laugh together, and cry together.[28] In addition to this, they enter into a partnership in which they run a joint home, manage their money together, and share the responsibility of raising their children.[29] In other words, marriage is not just escaping from loneliness— it's a "task."[30] If overcoming loneliness is one's only reason or motivation for marriage, chances are high that this reason alone will not sustain a long-lasting relationship.[31]

Social Pressure vs. Readiness and Personal Conviction

Social pressure has come to be one of the basic reasons why some people enter into marriage today. Society views marriage as very important, and it is often seen as abnormal for anyone not to marry. An unmarried adult past thirty years of age will often find himself or herself the object of well-meaning friends' pity or attempts at matchmaking.[32] This can be irritating and insulting to many single persons who have chosen either not to marry or to delay marriage.[33]

Also, society sees a married person as an adult who deserves the respect of society. It is unfortunate that single persons are often not perceived as adults in the same way their married peers are.[34] Therefore, because of the desire to earn the respect of society, to gain adult status and to avoid pity from family and friends, many people have entered into marriage prematurely only to find out that they were not yet ready. Readiness simply means to be prepared for what one is about to do. Marriage requires emotional, financial, and mental readiness. Individuals entering into marriage should be very careful not to substitute social pressures for readiness and personal conviction, which are very crucial in the choice of marriage. Marriage built on social pressures is undoubtedly on shaky ground. God's plan is for us is to have a lasting union built on personal readiness and conviction in the will of God and the leading of the Holy Spirit.

It is very sad and unfortunate that the understanding and continuing communion in affection for one another in marriage has been thrown out and what is left is selfishness and personal gratification.[35] Marriage and the rearing of a family is humanity's most important and sacred relationship, and it calls for a man and a woman who are dedicated to each other.[36] It is my prayer that we would have the right focus as we plan to enter into this great institution called marriage.

End Notes

[1] Stephen A. Grunlan, *Marriage and the Family*, (Grand Rapids, Michigan: Zondervan Publishing House, 1984), 92.

[2] Ibid., 128.

[3] Wood, *Marriage Readiness*, 23.

[4] Ibid.

[5] Mace, *Better Marriages*, 83.

[6] Lewis B. Smedes, *Sex for Christians* (Grand Rapids, Michigan: William B. Eerdmans Publishing Co., 1976), 96-97.

[7] Grunlan, *Marriage and the Family*, 72.

[8] Ibid, 73.

[9] Ibid, 74.

[10] Ibid.

[11] Paul Popenoe, *Sex, Love and Marriage* (New York City: Belmont Books, 1963), 94.

[12] Grunlan, *Marriage and the Family*, 94.

[13] Ibid, 95.

[14] Popenoe, *Sex, Love and Marriage*, 28-31.

[15] Ibid.

[16] Grunlan, *Marriage and the Family*, 111.

[17] Ibid.

[18] Smedes, *Sex for Christians*, 138.

[19] Ibid.

[20] Smedes, *Sex for Christians*, 141.

21 Ibid.

22 Allbritton, *How to Get Married*, 9.

23 Ibid.

24 Grunlan, *Marriage and the Family*, 111.

25 Grunlan, *Marriage and the Family*, 112.

26 Ibid.

27 Ibid, 94.

28 Mace, *We Can Have Better Marriages*, 71.

29 Mace, *We Can Have Better Marriages*, 71.

30 Ibid.

31 Grunlan, *Marriage and the Family*, 94.

32 Ibid, 95.

33 Ibid.

34 Ibid.

35 Paul Tournier, *To Understand Each Other* (Atlanta, Georgia: John Knox Press, 1967), 45.

36 Fred M. Wood, *Growing A Life Together* (Nashville, Tennessee: Broadman Press, 1975), 10.

4

Fundamentals of Interpersonal Relationships

We are living in a dynamic world of interactions and relationships. A world that yearns for and seeks friendships. Indeed, the significance of interpersonal relationships cannot be overemphasized. It is undoubtedly a vital part of human existence. While some people are quick to make friends, others are slow. However, it is important to note, according to Ernest White, that "we live and move and have our being in relationships—the most important of which is our relationship with God."[1]

Considering the fact that relationships are an important part of life, it is therefore relevant to say that learning the art of human relations cannot be considered an open elective—it is the course for the core of life.[2] Every worthwhile relationship, particularly marital union, must rest upon solid and genuine interpersonal relationships. I have written this section to present a theory of interpersonal relationships.

The chapter is divided into four parts; the first part deals with what an interpersonal relationship is; the second with theological reflection on interpersonal relationships; the third explains what I consider to be the process of interpersonal relationships; and the fourth concludes with the implications of the theory for personal ministry practice. Life is full of interpersonal relationships, and it is through coordination, patience, and self-giving that we may achieve action.[3]

What is an Interpersonal Relationship?

An interpersonal relationship, in the context of this book, will be defined as the state of being related or interrelated to one another as persons.[4] It may be used to describe a variety of friendships, from casual acquaintances to intimate relationship.[5] However, interpersonal relationship refers to a loving, personal, and caring relationship with attributes such as reciprocity, mutual choice, trust, loyalty, and openness.[6] Indeed, an interpersonal relationship becomes reliable and meaningful when the persons involved are able to demonstrate to one another both by words and actions that they, in fact, care for one another.

The deep urge within human beings to get close to one another[7] cannot be overemphasized. It makes interpersonal relationships more dynamic and compelling. Hence, in order to live in the world of interactions and friendships in interpersonal relationships, we must develop the capacity to love and also to be loved.

The Divine Call

A Theological Reflection on Interpersonal Relationships

But you are a chosen people, a royal priesthood, a holy nation, a people belonging to God, that you may declare the praises of him who called you out of darkness into his wonderful light (1 Peter 2:9).

Under the new covenant, a new relationship was established between God and the Church. The Church became the chosen people saved by grace and serving as priests to lead those in darkness to the light of the saving grace of Jesus Christ. Martin J. Heinecken, writing on the theology of Søren Kierkegaard, insisted that a man's eternal blessedness depends upon his or her relationship with the man, Jesus, His birth, death, and resurrection.[9] Also, J. Robert Nelson, writing on the theology of Emil Brunner, maintained that the truth about the Lord is discovered not through theorizing on His nature, but through a personal encounter or a relationship with Him.[10] Indeed, every Christian has been called into a personal relationship with God through Jesus Christ. And with Anna Polcino quoted by Ernest White in his book, *The Art of Human Relations,* we understand that "of all our relationships, the most important one is with God"[11] because it forms the basis for other relationships. It determines the quality of interpersonal relationships.[12]

Our sense of being and worth is derived from our relationship with God, and it is through this relationship that we can relate better in our interpersonal relationships. Our relationships with others will become meaningful and uplifting when they flow from our relationships with our friend Christ Jesus who willingly lay down His life for us (John 15:13). Jesus, in His call for a deeper or intimate relationship, said, *"I am the vine, you are the branches. If a man remains in me and I in him, he will bear much fruit; apart from me, you can do nothing"* (John 15:5). Truly our friendship with Christ is the first priority;[13] it helps define the quality of our interpersonal relationships, particularly in marital union.

The Process of Interpersonal Relationships

An interpersonal relationship is a process. It is always changing, always growing, and always in the process of becoming. When a relationship ceases to grow, the end result may be death; in other words, the relationship may cease to exist. Therefore, because of the dynamic nature of interpersonal relationships, I have used the word *process* to describe some key factors in interpersonal relationships.

An Interpersonal Relationship is Loving

Dear friends, let us love one another, for love comes from God. Everyone who loves has been born of God and knows God. Whoever does not love, does not know God, because God is love (John 4:7-8).

Love is the identifying characteristic of the Christian life, and it comes from God, who is love.[14] Jesus Christ said, *"A new command I give you: Love one another as I have loved you...By this, all men will know that you are my disciples, if you love one another"* (John 13:34-35). The word used here for love is *agape,* which means a self-giving love that seeks the best interest of another and is not selfish or self-seeking.[15] I am persuaded that self-giving love is a vital ingredient in interpersonal relationships. It is the shield that provides protection and comfort in times of weakness. It is the anchor that holds relationships in times of conflicts and misunderstandings. Without self-giving love, it may be difficult for interpersonal relationships to survive.

The world is dying for a little bit of love; everywhere we hear the sighing for a little bit of love.[16] There is nothing more thrilling or important than when these three words, "I love you," are spoken and lived in an interpersonal relationship.[17] Christian love in personal relationships is a response to God's infinite love.[18] Our love to God is demonstrated in the giving and sharing of ourselves with others in interpersonal relationships. There is surely nothing that is more at the core of any relationships than the realization of how friends really need to die to themselves if they are to give life to one another.[19] The Apostle Paul gave a beautiful illustration of the kind of love than can sustain interpersonal relationships when he wrote,

Love is patient, love is kind. It does not envy, it does not boast, it is not proud. It is not rude, it is not self-seeking, it is not easily angered, it keeps no record of wrongs. Love does not delight in evil but rejoices with the truth. It always protects, always trusts, always hopes, always perseveres. Love never fails (1 Corinthians 13:4-8).

In essence, an interpersonal relationship is loving and caring for one another. Lucas said,

"A relationship will grow whenever one person demonstrates to another both by his actions and his words that he respects the other, that he has concern for him and cares about what happens to him, and that he is willing both to listen and to act helpfully."[20]

We are called to love one another. This is what makes an interpersonal relationship worthwhile.

An Interpersonal Relationship is Trusting

Also fundamental to lasting interpersonal relationships is the joy of trusting one another. Like plants and other living things, an interpersonal relationship must have a conducive atmosphere in which to live and grow,[21] and one of the vital ingredients of this conducive atmosphere is trust. It is the channel that connects people in a relationship.[22] It makes a relationship dependable, and it encourages people to invest themselves in a relationship without fear.[23] Without trust, an interpersonal relationship becomes nothing but a mere game, shrouded in superficiality and insecurity. Dependable, honest, and faithful behaviors and actions are required if trust is to develop and grow in a relationship.[24]

Jeanie Miley, in her book, *Creative Silence*, wrote,

> "If it's difficult to fall back into the arms of waiting humans, or to allow oneself to be carried through strange territory by unnamed friends, of course it is difficult to fall back in the arms of God unless you practice that surrender, that trust, as a discipline of love in mediation."[25]

The same thing can be said of interpersonal relationships. I strongly believe that we cannot risk to fall into the arms of a person, especially in a relationship situation, without the willingness to trust the person. Trust grows within a relationship when we begin to risk with others and confirm them as human beings.[26] When trust is achieved in a relationship, it breeds commitment, unity, and connectedness. Indeed, living human beings and living human relationships require the ingredient of trust[27] if the relationships are to grow and survive.

An Interpersonal Relationship is Revealing

Writing on the issue of "solitude and silence," Dietrich Bonhoeffer said, "Let him who cannot be alone beware of community."[28] Following the same line of thought, I would say that let the person who is not willing to reveal himself and herself beware of interpersonal relationships. Self revealing is indeed another significant factor if an interpersonal relationship is to be genuine, meaningful, and trustworthy.

God is a revealing God. He makes Himself known to us through the prophets, the law, the scriptures, the Holy Spirit, and through nature and history.[29] His ultimate revelation was through the person of Jesus Christ, our Lord. He not only wanted us to have facts about Himself, but also to have personal and intimate knowledge of Him.[30] Therefore, to enter into an intimate relationship with God and our fellow human beings demands personal and self-revealing acts. Revealing is also self-disclosure, which simply means disclosing or revealing oneself.[31] It is to openly and non-apologetically reveal something somewhat private about ourselves.[32] It also means that we must have some knowledge of who we are and be willing for others to peek behind the curtains of our lives and see us the way we really are with all of our strengths and weaknesses.[33] Transparency is definitely an important ingredient of interpersonal relationships. The greater transparency a person practices, the more of himself or herself he or she reveals to another[34] and, more importantly, the more our interpersonal relationships grow.

An Interpersonal Relationship is Communicating

There is no doubt about the fact that many excellent books have been written on communication. This segment is just a brief explanation of the significance of effective communication in interpersonal relationships and, more importantly, in marital relationships. In the preceding discourse, we have examined the acts of loving, trusting, and revealing as significant factors in interpersonal relationships. Let us now try to understand another key element that is equally important to a healthy and lasting relationship, particularly in marriage. This key element is communicating.

Effective communication stimulates and motivates relationships. Communication is a part of life. Either we chose to speak or not; it must be understood that "all observable behavior is communication and can be considered a message."[35] Therefore, to build solid, intimate relationship, especially in marital union, we must endeavor to cultivate effective communication.

Interpersonal communication is defined to mean "the capacity to express feelings, beliefs, and desires of one person to another through verbal and non-verbal clues that are understood, acknowledged, and responded to by the recipient."[36] Lack of good communication may cripple a relationship. Thus, we must all learn how to transmit, decode, interpret, and respond to interpersonal communication in positive and reinforcing ways.[37]

As people living in relationships, we are always giving signals of some kind to persons with whom we interact.[38] Apparently, to strengthen our relationships, we have to understand what others are transmitting to us, as well as have them understand our messages.[39] Hence, in our striving for dynamic and lasting interpersonal relationships, we must learn to listen carefully to one another; we must be willing to risk openness, even when we become vulnerable, and we must try to clarify non-verbal signals.[40] In other words, we must learn to let our body language, feelings, and words agree, as we send out messages to another person.

Indeed, an interpersonal relationship is communicating. We must learn the art of communication if we are going to experience deep and meaningful relationships. In his book, *Strength in Servant Leadership,* Cedar said, "Loving and honest communication requires a great risk. I find that those I appreciate most are the people who love me enough to risk telling me the truth. They are my dearest, most trusted friends."[41] To maintain intimate interpersonal relationships, particularly in marriage, we must be willing to indulge in honest communication.

> *As the Father has loved me, so I have loved you...just as I have obeyed my Father's commands and remain in his love. I have told you this so that my joy may be in you and that your joy may be complete...Love each other as I have loved you* (John 15:9-12).

In this text, Jesus made it abundantly clear to His disciples that love should form the basis of their relationships with one another and also with those that would come to His saving grace through their message. Hence, in interpersonal relationship such as marital union, the eternal love of God must not just be a theory that people talk about; both wife and husband must live and practice it, for without it the union is destined to fail.

According to Gay and Kathlyn Hendricks, love is our glory, and it is also our power; it is so powerful that even a little of it can heal and transform lives permanently.[42] Also, in the words of McGinnis, "the best relationships are built up, like a fine lacquer finish with the accumulated layers of many acts of kindness."[43] In my view, the act of self-giving love in marital relationships through a life of obedience to the holy word of God and through the spirit of trusting, self-revealing, and honest communication will not only make Christian marriage strong and vibrant, it will make it worthwhile to the glory of God.

End Notes

[1] Ernest White, *The Art of Human Relations* (Nashville: Broadman Press, 1985), 71.

[2] Ibid, 13.

[3] Raymond S. Ross and Mark G. Ross, *Relating and Interacting: An Introduction to Interpersonal Communication* (New York: Prentice-Hall, Inc., 1982), 6.

[4] Merriam A. Webster, *Webster's Ninth New Collegiate Dictionary* (Massachusetts: Merriam Webster, Inc. 1987), 994.

[5] Susan A. Basow, *Gender Stereotypes: Tradition and Alternatives* (California: Brooks-Cole Publishing Company, 1986), 201.

[6] Ibid.

[7] Gay and Kathlyn Hendricks, *Centering and the Art of Intimacy* (New Jersey: Prentice-Hall, Inc., 1985), 13.

[8] All Scriptures quoted are taken from the New International Version (NIV) of the Bible, unless otherwise noted.

[9] Dean G. Peerman and Martin E. Marty, *A Handbook on Christian Theologians* (Nashville: Abingdon Press, 1965), 131.

[10] Ibid, 416.

[11] White, *Human Relations,* 23.

[12] Ibid, 23.

[13] Jeanie Miley, *Creative Silence: Keys to Deeper Life* (Dallas: Word Publishing, 1989), 32.

[14] *Disciples' Study Bible, New International Version,* Commentary on 1 John 4:7-21, 1619.

[15] Ibid.

[16] Henry Allen Parker, *Living at Peace in a Turbulent World* (Nashville: Broadman Press, 1973), 9.

[17] Ibid.

[18] John Powell, *Why Am I Afraid to Love* (Niles, Illinois: Argus Communications Company, 1967), 11.

[19] Eugene C. Kennedy, *A Time for Love* (New York: Image Books, 1970), 84.

[20] Alan Keith-Lucas, *Giving and Taking Help* (Chapel Hill: The University of North Carolina Press, 1972), 48-49.

[21] White, *Human Relations*, 153.

[22] Ibid, 164.

[23] Ibid.

[24] Ibid, 165.

[25] Miley, *Creative Silence*, 55.

[26] Richard L. Weaver II, *Understanding Interpersonal Communication* (London: Scott, Foresman, and Company, 1990), 119.

[27] White, *Human Relations*, 165.

[28] Dietrich Bonhoeffer, *Life Together* (New York: Harper and Row Publishers, 1954), 77.

[29] Doran C. McCarty, *The Inner Heart of Ministry* (Nashville: Broadman Press, 1985), 95.

[30] Ibid., 96.

[31] Weaver, *Understanding*, 109.

[32] Joseph M. Strayhorn, Jr., *Talking It Out: A Guide to Effective Communication and Problem Solving* (Illinois: Research Press Company, 1977), p. 34.

[33] McCarthy, *Inner Heart*, 100.

[34] White, *Human Relations*, 161.

[35] Weaver, *Understanding*, 24.

[36] John C. Howell, *Christian Marriage: Growing in Oneness* (Nashville: Convention Press, 1983), 55.

[37] Howell, *Christian Marriage*, 56.

[38] Ibid., 55.

[39] Ibid., 55-56.

[40] Ibid., 67-68.

[41] Paul A. Cedar, *Strength in Servant Leadership* (Waco: Word Books, Publishers, 1987) 55.

42 Hendricks, *Centering*, vii.

43 Alan Loy McGinnis, *The Friendship Factor* (Minneapolis: Augsburg Publishing House, 1979), 51.

Conclusion

I would love to conclude this book with these words of wisdom from an unknown author, which I think speaks volume concerning the aim and goal of this book.

The oneness of the husband and the wife
is a type of Christ and the church.
With Christ having preeminence over all things
is the glory between the couples.
Praying and studying the word in one accord
is the daily necessity.
Submission in the wife and love in the husband
is the basic rule for all daily walk.
Mutual honoring and care
is the expression of love.
Respect for each other's kinfolks
is the duty that brings blessings.
"Thank you" and "I'm sorry"
are words that ought to frequent the mouth.
Letting down on courtesy because of familiarity

is the beginning of discord.
The first occurrence of discord
is an opening for Satan's intrusion.
Speaking to others the shortcomings of their partner
provides further opportunities for Satan's malice.
Counting your partner's shortcomings
and dwelling on your own virtues
are invitations to Satan's suggestions.
Never allowing yourself to be the other's cross
while remembering that the other is always your cross
is the secret to victory.

Appendix A

Some Learning Tools and Skills for Lasting and Fulfilling Marriage

These learning tools and skills are selections from materials used in marriage conferences and seminars I have had the opportunity of leading over the years. I pray that these materials will be of great blessing to you and your marriage.

Take Me and My Marriage to the Cross

The cross is an emblem of sacrifice, redemption, and restoration. And marriage is not a human concept. Dr. Myles Munroe, the author of *Understanding Love*, said,

> "Mankind did not simply dream up marriage somewhere along the line as a convenient way of handling relationships and responsibilities between men and women or dealing with child-bearing and parenting issues. Marriage is of divine origin."

God created and ordained the institution of marriage. Marriage is the deepest and most intimate of all human relationships. Thus, if you are looking forward to an enduring and lasting marriage, you must take your marriage to the cross.

For it is at the cross that fellowship with God was restored.

For he himself is our peace, who has made the two one and has destroyed the barrier, the dividing wall of hostility, by abolishing in his flesh the law with its commandments and regulations. His purpose was to create in himself one new man out of the two, thus making peace, and in this one body to reconcile both of them to God through the cross, by which he put to death their hostility (Ephesians 2:14-16).

For God was pleased to have all his fullness dwell in him, and through him to reconcile to himself all things, whether things on earth or things in heaven, by making peace through his blood, shed on the cross (Colossians 1:19-20).

For it is at the cross that the bond and the yoke of eternal death was broken.

When the LORD goes through the land to strike down the Egyptians, he will see the blood on the top and sides of the doorframe and will pass over that doorway, and he will not permit the destroyer to enter your houses and strike you down (Exodus 12:23).

Whoever believes in him is not condemned, but whoever does not believe stands condemned already because he has not believed in the name of God's one and only Son (John 3:18).

Whoever believes in the Son has eternal life, but whoever rejects the Son will not see life, for God's wrath remains on him (John 3:36).

I tell you the truth, whoever hears my word and believes him who sent me has eternal life and will not be condemned; he has crossed over from death to life (John 5:24).

Blessed and holy are those who have part in the first resurrection. The second death has no power over them, but they will be priests of God and of Christ and will reign with him for a thousand years (Revelation 20:6).

For it is at the cross that the power of the evil one was crushed.

When you were dead in your sins and in the uncircumcision of your sinful nature, God made you alive with Christ. He forgave us all our sins, having canceled the written code, with its regulations, that was against us and that stood opposed to us; he took it away, nailing it to the cross. And having disarmed the powers and authorities, he made a public spectacle of them, triumphing over them by the cross (Colossians 2:13-15).

For it is at the cross that abundant life is given to anyone who chooses to come to the cross.

The thief comes only to steal and kill and destroy; I have come that they may have life, and have it to the full [abundantly] (John 10:10).

Abundant life is a life filled with:

* The presence of God;
* The love of God;
* The favor and mercy of God;
* The comfort of God;
* The strength of God for the journey;
* Satisfaction, contentment, and fulfillment; and
* Purpose and self-giving.

Some Keys to An Enduring and Peaceful Marital Union

Recognize God's authorship of your marriage.
Be determined to build your marriage.
Humble yourself under the mighty hands of God.
Don't think too highly of yourself; don't be selfish or self centered (Philippians 2:5-8; 1 Corinthians 4:7).
Seek always the good of your mate (Philippians 2:3-4).
Use your tongue to edify (Ephesians 4:29).

What Do I Believe and Live By?

A worldview is the framework from which we view reality and make sense of life and the world. What you believe and live by:

* Forms the basis of who you are;
* Helps set your priorities in life;
* Will determine the kind of person you allow into your life, the kind of association you align yourself with, etc.

Some biblical framework from which we view reality:

* What kind of faith is your faith?
* What is your view of God?
* What is your view of God's word?
* What is your view of stewardship and possessions?
* What is your view of holy and righteous living?
* What is your understanding of the leadership of the Holy Spirit?

The Power of the Cross in Your Marriage

Burdens are lifted at Calvary (spiritual, emotional, and physical).
Forgiveness is appreciated and celebrated.
Loving your spouse becomes sacrificial.
The unity of your marriage will be strengthened.
Strengthens family altar.

Make Unity Your Goal: the Oneness Principle
A) Through:

* Leaving, cleaving, and becoming (Genesis 2:18-25). Oneness or unity is described in three vital levels of relationship development. These three

levels were so important to God that they were mentioned four different times in scripture (Genesis 2:24; Matthew 19:5; Mark 10:7-8; and Ephesians 5:31).

* Mutual submission (Ephesians 5:21).
* Self-giving love.
* Complete openness.
* Trust and faithfulness.
* The discipline of humility (Proverbs 3:34; 1 Peter 5:5).

B) Pray for Unity (The Lord Jesus prayed for unity: John 17:13-23)

C) Make unity your choice and be determined to keep it.

E) Be careful of the little foxes. (Song of Songs 2:15)

D) Be mindful of the devil's schemes (Matthew 26:41; 1 Peter 5:8).

F) Maintaining financial unity.

What we are and everything we have come from God (Psalm 24:1; 1 Chronicles 29:11,14). God is the one who gives us the grace to work and make money (Deuteronomy 8:18; 1 Chronicles 29:11,12; Proverbs 10:22; 1 Corinthians 4:7).

But remember the LORD your God, for it is he who gives you the ability to produce wealth, and so confirms his covenant, which he swore to your forefathers, as it is today (Deuteronomy 8:18).

Yours, O LORD, is the greatness and the power and the glory and the majesty and the splendor, for everything in heaven and earth is yours. Yours, O LORD, is the kingdom; you are exalted as head over all (1 Chronicles 29:11).

Wealth and honor come from you; you are the ruler of all things. In your hands are strength and power to exalt and give strength to all (1 Chronicles 29:12).

The blessing of the LORD brings wealth, and he adds no trouble to it (Proverbs 10:22).

For who makes you different from anyone else? What do you have that you did not receive? And if you did receive it, why do you boast as though you did not? (1 Corinthians 4:7).

We are stewards of all that we have: Thus, we must use our financial resources prayerfully and carefully, as He desires not as you desire (Matthew 25:14-30). For it is required in stewards that a man be found faithful (1 Corinthians 4:2). "Unity" or the "one-flesh" principle includes the financial aspect of marriage. (Genesis 2:24).

Marriage is a total commitment and a total sharing of your total person with another person until death. And included in the total sharing is the financial aspect of marriage (Wayne Mack). Money must not be allowed to stand as a hindrance against the unity and oneness in marriage.

Principles of Money Management

* Amount of money is not as important as how it is managed.

* Do not make money your God (*"The love of money..."* 1 Timothy 6:10).

* Husband and wife must view money as "family's money," not "my money" or "your money."

* Use credit wisely.

* Endeavor to live within your income (Proverbs 22:7).

* Develop a financial plan (budget) acceptable to both partners.

Experiencing Deep Intimacy in your Marriage

* Trust bond must be preserved and maintained: "Trust is never something that is earned once and for all; it's something that is warranted by consistent honor and care toward each other" (*HomeLife:* Learning to Trust Again Sept. p. 14).

* Complete openness (Genesis 2:24-25).

* The feeling of security.

* Celebrate the worth and value of your spouse.

* Negative assumptions about your mate (Philippians 4:8).

Ten Biblical Love Languages in Marriage

(1 Peter 3:7; Colossians 3:18,19; Ephesians 5:25,28; Matthew 7:24; 1 Corinthians 13:4-8)

* Choice: Love is a choice.
* Honor/Respect
* Faithfulness/Honesty
* Commitment
* Submission
* Trust
* Patience
* Forgiveness
* Openness
* Financial Integrity/Trustworthiness

Five Emotional Love Languages in Marriage

The emotional climate of your marriage is vital to the survival of your marriage. A healthy emotional atmosphere will breathe freshness and vitality into your marriage; your love for each other will be enhanced.

* Words of affirmation (Proverbs 18:21; 12:25).
* Quality time with one another: giving your undivided attention to your spouse.
* Symbolic expressions of love: giving and receiving gifts.
* Acts of self-giving service: *"Serve one another in love"* (John 13:3-17; Galatians 5:13).
* Physical touch (Mark 10:13; 10:14-16).

Some Traits of a Healthy Christian Family

Christ centered.

Shares a common value deeply rooted in Christ.

Affirms and supports one another.

Shares self-giving and unconditional love.

Turns conflict into blessings.

There is a sense of trust.

Openness is celebrated in the oneness of fellowship.

Reliant on the strength of family altar.

Communicates and listens.

Honors and respects one another.

Man's View of Marriage

* Contract
* Convenience
* Temporary
* Self-Gratification
* Feeling based

God's View of Marriage

* Covenant
* Commitment
* Permanency
* Self-Giving
* Responsibility

When the Child Comes

Receive the child as a precious gift given by God to bless and strengthen the tie that binds you and your spouse in the bond of marriage.

The child should not become an obstacle that separates but a special blessing that strengthens the oneness principle in marriage.

Always remember that you and your spouse were first together before the child came.

Prioritize in a healthy and balanced manner your attention between your spouse and your child.

Don't lose focus on your fellowship and intimacy with your spouse.

Celebrating the Gift of Sexual Union in Marriage

Oneness in a general or broader sense involves the totality of a shared life in marriage. However, there is no place where this total sharing is more beautifully pictured or fully experienced than in the celebration of sexual union between a wife and a husband in the union of marriage.

A. Sexual bond is a gift from god.

B. Sexual relations in marriage is holy and good (Hebrews 13:4).

C. Sex in marriage is designed by God for pleasure (Proverbs 5:18, 19; Song of Songs 4:10-12).

D. Sex in marriage was designed by God for procreation (Genesis 1:28; Deuteronomy 7:13,14; Psalm 127:3; 139:13-15).

E. Sex in marriage is a form of communication of our deepest affection—the blending of spirit, mind, and soul (Genesis 2:24).

F. Sex in marriage should be received with thanksgiving.

G. Sex in marriage is not performance centered, it is self-giving centered (Song of Songs 6:3).

Beware of the Little Foxes That May Destroy and Strangle Your Marriage and Your Sexual Intimacy (1 Corinthians 13:4-7, Song of Songs 2:15):

* Anger
* Rudeness
* Pride
* Self-seeking attitude
* Unforgiving spirit
* Foolish talk
* Nagging spirit
* Ungrateful heart

Reclaiming Your Marriage

Renew your personal relationship with the Lord through repentance and total obedience to God's will.

Receive your marriage as a precious gift from God (Song of Songs 4:7).

Daily lift your marriage before the throne of grace and mercy.

Say to the evil one, "You have no place in my marriage."

Showing Forgiveness

* Forgiveness may be defined as letting go of any wrong done to you. This is letting go of the need for vengeance and every associated feeling, such as bitterness and resentment.

* It is a command from the Lord.

* It has no limitation (Luke 17:3).

* It strengthens the oneness principle. Intimacy is enhanced and empowered in forgiveness.

* It strengthens the family altar.

* It strengthens your spiritual well-being.

* It strengthens your psychological well-being (emotional)

* You will also receive forgiveness

The Power of Appreciation in Marriage

Appreciation is an essential part of human relationships, especially marital union. As important as this principle is, it is rarely used. Many couples resort to destructive instead of constructive criticism.

Appreciation (noun) is defined as an expression of admiration, approval, or gratitude. It is an act of kindness to another.

A) It strengthens the communion between the couple.

B) It honors individual values of the couple.

C) It increases the level of joy and celebration between the couple.

D) It helps to build up the individuals.

E) It encourages willingness for service without tears.

Living in Peace and Joy with a Difficult Spouse

Case Study: 1 Samuel 25

A) Marriage as ordained by God is the highest relationship possible among men. It is intended by God:

* To complement;

*To be peaceful and joyful;

* To be satisfying;

* To be fulfilling; and

* To be a permanent and lasting union.

But some marriages, particularly among believers, can be very painful and some may even be considered to be a hell on earth. And this is because God's ordained purpose for marriage has been strangled by the stubbornness of a spouse who blatantly continues to disregard the leadership of the Holy Spirit.

The question is, how can one live in this situation and still maintain a sense of joy and peace in the soul?

B) Some Challenges of a Difficult Spouse

* Spouse Mismatch: *Type One*—a believer getting married to an unbeliever, a clear violation of Gods will; *Type Two*—two unbelieving people, one spouse saved after marriage.

* Level of spiritual maturity.
* Some habits that are considered annoying by the other spouse: not organized, forgetful, does not want to lead or pray with the family, withdrawal or silence in the face of confrontation, gets angry easily etc.
* Obstinate attitude.
* Making rash decisions not based on the full counsel of God.
* Ungodly influence.
* A distorted view of financial matters (world view versus Biblical view).
* Hard to talk to: cannot have a dialogue without resulting in a shouting match.
* Good and amiable outside but hostile at home.
* Has no desire to change.

C) Some Coping Skills

Instead of focusing on your struggles, fix your eyes on the Lord.
He deserves your primary allegiance.
Make God the center of your life.
He is able to meet needs that your spouse never could.
He is able to empower you to love your spouse when he or she is not very lovable.
He can create something good from a painful union.
He will be your spouse when your earthly spouse is distant.
God loves your partner more than you do.

Make your spouse the number one human being in your life.

Love your spouse unconditionally.

Acknowledge the failings of your spouse.

Know that God is the one that is ultimately able to change and impact the life of your spouse: don't try to bear the burden by yourself.

Focus on, appreciate, and celebrate the good qualities of your spouse.

Respect and honor your spouse.

Be determined to make your marriage work.

Create a positive and nurturing environment for your children.

Pray without ceasing.

Seek the support of a godly counsel.

Take advantage of the support system your church may have.

Appendix B

Conference for the Singles

These are some of the issues discussed in some of my conferences for the singles. And I pray it would be a source of blessing to those who are planning and seeking to enter into this great institution of marriage.

Some of the themes used in some of these conferences are "Looking Forward for A Home Whose Builder and Maker is the Lord (Hebrews 11:10)"; "The Joy of Singleness (2 Corinthians 7:6-9)"; and "According to the Counsel of His Will (Ephesians 1:11)"

A) This conference is based on the following convictions:

That singleness is a season of life in God's plan;

That singleness can be fulfilling;

That singleness is a gift;

That singleness is a choice; and

That singleness can lead to deeper relationship with God.

B) This conference is designed to strengthen and empower singles in:

Their walk of faith with the Lord;

Their interpersonal relationships;

Their desire for and choice of partner in marriage;

Experiencing the joy of singleness; and

Their Christian service unto the Lord.

C) Some basic issues from the conferences:

Seven misconceptions about singleness;

Singles are more unfulfilled than married couples;

Marriage solves all the problems of singleness;

Marriage is God's highest calling;

Singles struggle with loneliness more than married people;

Singles have more time and money;

Singles are more self-centered; and

Singles are more sexually frustrated.

Seven Unhealthy Motivations for Marriage:

Parental pressure;

Societal and peer pressures;

Rescue fantasies;

Pregnancy;

Seeking sexual passion;

Escape fantasy; and

The wish for security (seeking someone to provide financial and emotional security).

Seven Healthy Factors for Christian Marital Union

Genuine desire to enter a covenantal marital union;
Self-giving love;
Reliance on the will of God;
Readiness;
Inner man or beauty based on Christian virtues but not merely on outward man or beauty;
Marriage is the celebration of communion;
The prayer factor;

Celebrating the joy of singleness;

Accept your season of singleness as a passage of life;
Maintain a sense of purpose and direction—don't put your life on hold until Mr. or Miss Right comes along;
Be content with who you are in God's plan;
Look for opportunities to serve God through your local church and community; and
Cultivate the friendship and fellowship of others in a loving and caring church.

Resources

Allbritton, Cliff. *How To Get Married and Stay That Way.* Nashville, Tennessee: Broadman Press, 1982.

Basow, Susan A. *Gender Stereotypes: Traditions and Alternatives.* Monterey: Brooks/Cole Publishing Company, 1986.

Bonhoeffer, Dietrich. *Life Together.* New York: Harper and Row, Publishers, 1954.

Cedar, Paul A. *Strength In Servant Leadership.* Waco: Work Books, Publishers, 1987.

Disciple's Study Bible, New International Version.

Githumbi, Kamau Wa, et al., eds. *Marriage Before and After.* Achimota, Ahana: African Christian Press, 1982.

Grunlan, Stephen A. *Marriage and the Family.* Grand Rapids, Michigan: Zondervan Publishing House, 1984.

Hendricks, Gay and Kathlyn. *Centering and the Art of Intimacy.* New Jersey: Prentice-Hall, Inc., 1985.

Howell, John C. *Christian Marriage: Growing in Oneness.* Nashville: Convention Press, 1983.

Kennedy, Eugene C. *A Time for Love*. New York: Image Books—A division of Doubleday and Company, Inc., 1970.

Lucas-Keith, Alan. *Giving and Taking Help*. Chapel Hill: The University of North Carolina Press, 1972.

Mace, David and Vera. *We Can Have Better Marriages If We Really Want Them*. New York: Abingdon Press, 1974.

McCarty, Doran C. *The Inner Heart of Ministry*. Nashville: Broadman Press, 1985.

McGinnis, Alan Loy. *The Friendship Factor*. Minneapolis: Augsburg Publishing House, 1979.

Miley, Jeanie. *Creative Silence: Keys to the Deeper Life*. Dallas: Word Publishing, 1989.

Parker, Henry Allen. *Living at Peace in a Turbulent World*. Nashville: Broadman Press, 1973.

Peerman, Dean G., and Marty, Martin E., eds. *A Handbook of Christian Theologians*. Nashville: Abingdon Press, 1984.

Popenoe, Paul. *Sex, Love and Marriage*. New York City: Belmont Books, 1963.

Powell, John. *Why Am I Afraid to Love?* Niles, Illinois: Argus Communications Company, 1967.

Ross, Raymond S., and Ross, Mark G. *Relating and Interacting: An Introduction to Interpersonal Communication*. New Jersey: Prentice-Hall, Inc., 1982.

Smedes, Lewis B. *Sex For Christians.* Grand Rapids, Michigan: William B. Eerdmans Publishing Company, 1976.

Strayhorn, Joseph M., Jr. *Talking It Out: An Guide to Effective Communication and Problem Solving.* Champaign, Illinois: Research Press Company, 1977.

Tournier, Paul. *To Understand Each Other.* Atlanta, Georgia: John Knox Press, 1967.

Weaver, Richard L. II. *Understanding Interpersonal Communication.* Fifth Edition. Glenview, Illinois: Scott, Foresman, and Company, 1990.

Webster, Merriam A. *Webster's Ninth New Collegiate Dictionary.* Springfield: Merriam Webster Inc., Publishers, 1987.

White, Ernest. *The Art of Human Relations.* Nashville: Broadman Press, 1985.

Wood, Fred M. *Growing a Life Together.* Nashville, Tennessee: Belmont Books, 1963.